COVER **TO** | BI[...]
7 SE[...]
AN[...]

Elijah

A MAN AND HIS GOD

CWR

Christopher Brearley

Contents

Introduction

The appearance of Elijah on the stage of history is dramatic. He confronts King Ahab and says, 'As the LORD, the God of Israel, lives, whom I serve, there will be neither dew nor rain in the next few years except at my word' (1 Kings 17:1). One sentence is spoken, containing an oath and a threat, and then he leaves.

Where did Elijah confront Ahab? Did he challenge him as the king was going around his kingdom? Did he walk unheralded into his court? It is not possible to say. Neither do we know anything of his ancestry or early life other than that he came from Tishbe in Gilead, a wild and rugged area east of the Jordan. What is clear, however, is that God used Elijah to counter the increasing unbelief and idolatry of the northern kingdom of Israel and lead the people back to true worship.

In 1 Kings 15:25–16:34 are described the reigns of six of Israel's kings. It is a very depressing story. They all disregarded God and His laws, and their evil example was readily followed by the vast majority of their subjects. Ahab, the last of these kings, was worse than those before him. To form a political alliance he married Jezebel, the daughter of King Ethbaal of the Sidonians, and he began to worship Baal. This was a clear violation of the first commandment: 'You shall have no other gods before me' (Exod. 20:3).

It should not be assumed that Ahab worshipped Baal only. He and many of his subjects believed that it was possible to worship both Baal and God. The former was recognised as the god who controlled the weather and fertility, whilst everything else could be assigned to the God of their fathers. This attitude was nothing new, for the worship of Baal had existed before Ahab's reign (Judg. 2:11,13; 1 Sam. 12:10). But Ahab gave it official sanction.

Jezebel had far greater religious convictions than her husband and was determined to substitute the Canaanite god Baal, and its associated sexual immorality, in place of the true God. She was totally committed to this and would not be content until all rivals were eradicated. Ahab, a weak man in a position of power, was content to acquiesce and became a puppet in her hands. Consequently, she established idolatry in Israel on a grand scale, maintaining 450 prophets of Baal plus 400 prophets of the goddess Asherah. Shrines and temples arose throughout the nation in honour of these false deities, whilst the altars of the God of Israel, like that at Carmel (1 Kings 18:30), were destroyed. Furthermore, Jezebel was killing the Lord's prophets. Such was the woman whose anger Elijah faced.

The abandonment of the true God was so bad during Ahab's reign that Hiel, a man from Bethel, was allowed to rebuild the walls of Jericho. God had said they were never to be rebuilt (Josh. 6:26). As a result Hiel paid a heavy penalty for his defiance. At the commencement of the work his eldest son died. And when he completed the work, by setting up the gates, his youngest son died. The word of the Lord to Joshua was fulfilled!

Ahab and the nation were experiencing serious spiritual and moral decay. Not only was Baal widely worshipped, but God's Word was treated with contempt. How would God react? Into this situation He sent Elijah – his name means 'Jehovah is my God' – to radically change Israel's attitude towards false gods.

Some people would say, 'If only we had such gifted men and women of God today.' But such a desire is not impossible. Elijah, the Bible reveals, was just like us (James 5:17). His needs and reactions are typical of human nature in every generation. Therefore, it would be wrong to place him upon a pedestal and imagine him to be a demigod or someone who has set a standard that no one else can emulate. He was only a man. His life clearly reveals not what a great person can do for God, rather it is what God can achieve through an ordinary person who not only desires but also is determined to serve Him.

Where now is the Lord, the God of Elijah? That question was asked by Elijah's successor, Elisha (2 Kings 2:14). It is a vital question that needs to be asked today because our need of the Spirit's power to achieve what we could never achieve by ourselves has not changed. How do we react to the fact that Jesus is no longer on earth? Jesus said, 'You may ask me for anything in my name, and I will do it' (John 14:14). To claim this promise, however, our prayers must not be selfish but always in the interest of God's kingdom. Do we genuinely have the faith to believe that there is no problem which is too great?

Elijah prayed earnestly that no rain would fall, and none fell for the next three and a half years. Then he prayed for rain and down it poured, with the result that the land produced crops again. Admittedly Elijah was in some ways unique. He had a ministry for a specific time. Even so, there are many lessons that are applicable to all Christians. A careful study of the life of Elijah will prepare and enable us to effectively witness in a society that today is increasingly hostile, or indifferent, towards the worship of the true and living God. Therefore, are you ready for the first session of the study?

WEEK 1

God Provides for His People

Opening Icebreaker

An idol is anything that takes first place in a person's or nation's life instead of the living God. Discuss what you consider to be modern-day idols. How can they be avoided?

Bible Readings

- Exodus 20:1–6
- 1 Kings 16:29–17:16

Opening Our Eyes

Elijah told Ahab of the drought. Then the Lord told Elijah to go and hide (1 Kings 17:1–2). Why? Would it not have appeared more logical for him to proclaim the prophetic word of judgment to all who would listen? Or maybe he should have remained in Samaria to see if Ahab repented. Not so! Hiding Elijah from the scene of public action was a divine judgment on the nation. They would not only suffer physically, due to the drought, but also experience a spiritual famine through not hearing the words of the Lord. Years later, Amos prophesied another spiritual famine for the people of Israel (Amos 8:11–12). Additionally, Elijah's disappearance protected him from Ahab and Jezebel's anger and prepared him for his future ministry. By walking with God, one step at a time, he became the man God wanted him to be.

Elijah was commanded to follow certain directions and he would be provided for. So he did as the Lord had told him. He was going to be totally dependent on God for daily provision. This was to be the commencement of an ever-deepening relationship that would eventually enable him to triumph over the prophets of Baal on Mount Carmel.

Our responsibility, as Elijah's was, is to submit humbly to the Word of God. He orders and promises and we are to trust and obey. Only then can we successfully cope with life's difficulties and be a spiritual blessing to others.

Elijah was in the right place and God provided for him. He drank from the brook and ravens brought him bread and meat each morning and evening. No luxuries were provided but he had everything necessary to survive and certainly more than many who were living in Israel.

Having ravens come to feed him must at first have been exciting; though later it might have become monotonous. The Jews in the wilderness were excited when miraculously fed. However, that which was at first valuable to them (Exod. 16:20) is later contemptuously called 'this manna' (Num. 11:6). Do we sometimes feel that there is monotony in the Lord's blessings?

Initially Elijah also had to face intense loneliness. Like many people he had to learn to be alone with God. Furthermore he had to face a severe test of insecurity. He was by a brook, not a river, and each day the water level dropped perceptibly. The situation became increasingly desperate. Had he made a mistake in going there? What should he do? It's a tremendous test of character when even the bare necessities are shrinking. Elijah did not panic and remained until the brook dried up. Only then did the Lord tell him to go to Zarephath, near the city of Sidon. There a woman would feed him.

When Elijah eventually met this woman, who was a widow, she told a wretched story. All that she had was a handful of flour and a little cooking oil. She and her son were about to experience the slow death of starvation. Nevertheless she did as Elijah commanded and baked him a small cake of bread. As a result God's promise was fulfilled and every day, whilst the drought lasted, sufficient food was miraculously provided. Elijah learned to rely on God for all his physical needs. He also learned that God's work was not confined to Israel but included this heathen widow and her son. God will accept those from every nation who fear Him and do what is right.

Discussion Starters

1. Elijah followed God. How can we experience God's guidance?

_____
_____
_____
_____
_____

2. Why is absolute obedience important to our spiritual life?

_____
_____
_____
_____
_____

3. What does God promise to those – like Elijah – who obey?

_____
_____
_____
_____
_____

4. What does the Bible say about loneliness and also about the ability to be alone?

_____
_____
_____
_____
_____

5. Elijah was told to go and live in the village of
Zarephath. Why did God send him there?

_____

_____

_____

_____

_____

6. God often works in mysterious ways. What might
Elijah have considered to be illogical in his walk with
God?

_____

_____

_____

_____

_____

7. Elijah responded to the widow's plight by saying,
'... first make a small cake of bread for me from
what you have and bring it to me, and then make
something for yourself and your son.' What do we
learn from this?

_____

_____

_____

_____

_____

8. Can I trust God to supply my daily needs? Is Jesus
Christ God's provision for me?

_____

_____

_____

_____

_____

Personal Application

Elijah and the widow and her son each day had sufficient food for their needs. God deals with people daily. How could it be otherwise if we are to live by faith? In the prayer taught us by our Lord we pray, 'Give us today our daily bread' (Matt. 6:11). Also we are taught to pray for the basic necessities to sustain life, not for luxuries. Agur prayed, '... give me neither poverty nor riches, but give me only my daily bread. Otherwise, I may have too much and disown you and say, "Who is the LORD?" Or I may become poor and steal, and so dishonour the name of my God' (Prov. 30:8–9). Satan will tempt us to want more, but we, like Jesus, can resist him with the truth of God's Word.

Seeing Jesus in the Scriptures

Satan showed Jesus all the kingdoms of the world and their splendour. '"All this I will give to you," he said, "if you will bow down and worship me."' Jesus responded by saying, 'Away from me, Satan! For it is written: "Worship the Lord your God, and serve him only"' (Matt. 4:9–10). The answer quotes Deuteronomy 6:13.

Satan delights in making that which is sinful appear to be desirable. Hence, a common response is to yield to temptation and cling to worthless idols. Do we seek first God's kingdom and His righteousness? Do we trust God alone for all our needs?

WEEK 2

The Widow's Son

Opening Icebreaker

Identify the ways in which anger can affect our lives and what we should do about it. Is anger ever appropriate?

Bible Readings

- 1 Kings 17:17–24
- Luke 7:11–17

Opening Our Eyes

The widow did as Elijah said and God's promise was fulfilled. They had sufficient food for all their needs. Then, in the midst of this miracle, tragedy suddenly struck and the widow's son died. Obviously obedience to God's commands does not necessarily mean that life progresses according to our expectations. Understandably this creates a dilemma and raises many difficult questions. Why should God take the life of a boy who He had apparently promised to sustain until the famine was over? Is this how God repays those who help His servants? Or did God not have the power to fulfil His promise? How should a Christian respond when God appears to fail?

We expect the elderly to die, but the death of a child or a loved one who has unexpectedly and prematurely died is much more difficult to accept. What a severe and painful test this is. The widow's deep distress in the loss of her only child, her anger towards God and His prophet Elijah, was bitterly expressed in her comment: 'What do you have against me, man of God? Did you come to remind me of my sin and kill my son?' (1 Kings 17:18). Maybe she was to blame for something evil in her past. Even so, how could God be so cruel? All her expectations for the future were shattered.

There is no reference in the Bible that anyone had previously been raised from the dead. Therefore, how would Elijah react to this seemingly impossible situation? It is common when things go wrong to make excuses so as to evade responsibility. Adam's immediate response, when challenged by God for his sin, was to blame Eve, and such an attitude is prevalent in every generation. Commendably, Elijah did not try to justify himself. Rather he used the opportunity to display the abounding love and almighty power of his God.

The only thing you can do in what appears to be an unexplainable and irretrievable tragedy is to take it to God in prayer. This is what Elijah did and he was then to learn that the earnest prayer of a righteous person has great power. He stretched himself out over the child three times and cried out to the Lord that the child's life would be restored. The situation was so urgent that probably he would, if possible, have imparted his own life into the boy. Unhesitatingly he brought himself into contact with that which was considered defiled: 'Whoever touches the dead body of anyone will be unclean for seven days' (Num. 19:11). It was such deep compassion, centuries later, that caused Jesus to raise from the dead another widow's son (Luke 7:14–15).

Because of his faith and God's promise this prayer was answered. We can imagine the great joy of Elijah as he gave the boy back to his mother saying, 'Look, your son is alive!' (1 Kings 17:23). Delighted, she realised that God had heard Elijah's cry and so was able to say 'Now I know that you are a man of God and that the word of the LORD from your mouth is the truth.' Previously she had acknowledged that the God of Israel was Elijah's God and not her own (1 Kings 17:12). Now it was different, for she had seen the truth (v.24). Furthermore, Elijah could confidently leave the widow and, as an invincible man of God, successfully face many in the contest on Mount Carmel.

Discussion Starters

1. If God is good and all powerful, why does He allow the righteous to suffer? Think of some biblical examples.

   _____

   _____

   _____

   _____

   _____

2. How would you refute the argument that suffering is always due to the sin of the sufferers?

   _____

   _____

   _____

   _____

   _____

3. Do we ever judge God prematurely on the basis of outward appearances?

   _____

   _____

   _____

   _____

   _____

4. How do I stay close to God in times of difficulty?

   _____

   _____

   _____

   _____

5. Discuss the different reactions to the boy's death of the widow and Elijah.

_____

_____

_____

_____

_____

6. Elijah pleaded with God to restore the boy to life again. What primary reason had he to expect that his request would be granted?

_____

_____

_____

_____

7. Sometimes we pray and we don't seem to get an answer. Why not?

_____

_____

_____

_____

_____

8. What did God achieve by allowing the boy to die and then live again?

_____

_____

_____

_____

Personal Application

Elijah was just an ordinary man who prayed and extraordinary things happened. God always listens to and answers those who are sincere, though their requests may be denied. Always between the prayer and the answer is the sovereignty of God. Elijah did not receive everything he prayed for (1 Kings 19:4). Paul pleaded three times that his painful 'thorn in the flesh' would be removed. His earnest prayer request was refused. Instead God gave Paul the ability to bear it (2 Cor. 12:7–9). Paradoxically, sickness can be a blessing. We are not necessarily allowed to avoid difficulties but rather we are given the strength and wisdom to conquer them.

Seeing Jesus in the Scriptures

On three known occasions Jesus restored a dead person to life. These are the widow's only son (Luke 7:15), the ruler's daughter (Luke 8:55) and Lazarus (John 11:44). He was filled with compassion for them.

Elijah (1 Kings 17:20–22) and Elisha (2 Kings 4:32–35) agonisingly struggled to restore life whilst Jesus simply gave the command and it was done. The reason is that Jesus, who rose again from the dead, is God.

A time is coming when all the dead will be raised to life. The resurrection of believers will be blessed (Rev. 20:6), but the fate of unbelievers is condemnation (John 5:29). Those who trust in Jesus for forgiveness will inherit eternal life; others will rise again only to be condemned.

WEEK 3

Conflict on Carmel

Opening Icebreaker

Imagine yourself alongside Elijah when he pleaded with the Lord to restore a boy to life, prayed for fire and then for rain. What might you learn from the way he prayed?

Bible Readings

- 1 Kings 18:1–46
- Psalm 100 (an affirmation that the Lord alone is God)
- James 5:17–18

Opening Our Eyes

God commanded Elijah to leave Zarephath and return to Israel. He was to tell Ahab that the drought would soon end. Meanwhile, Ahab summoned Obadiah and said, 'We must search all the springs and valleys to see if we can find some grass to keep my horses and mules alive.' So they divided the land between them, Ahab going in one direction and Obadiah in another.

Obadiah was a man of fear. He had a fear of God and a fear of man. Whilst in charge of Ahab's palace he had used his authority to protect a hundred prophets of God. This required great courage, for Jezebel, had she known, would surely have had him killed. Nevertheless, despite being a devout believer, he was reluctant to do as Elijah commanded. He was afraid to face the king's fury until Elijah reassured him. Only then did Obadiah tell Ahab that Elijah had come, and Ahab went out to meet him. Did he go seeking forgiveness? No, Ahab was in no doubt that Elijah was responsible for the drought. He immediately said, 'Is that you, you troubler of Israel?' The trouble, however, was because of the sin of Ahab and the Israelites. In reality Elijah was Israel's friend, for anyone who prevents continuing sin is a blessing.

Elijah told Ahab to summon the people from all over Israel to meet him on Mount Carmel. Here he would publicly challenge the prophets of Baal and reveal who was the true God. The people had wavered for years between God and Baal, thus disobeying the first of the Ten Commandments (Exod. 20:3). The Lord alone was to be Israel's God. Even the severe drought had not convinced them to renounce Baal worship. Therefore, Elijah proposed a miraculous test. The god who answered by fire was the true God. All the people agreed that this was a good idea.

The Baal priests chose which bull they would use for the sacrifice, prepared it and called on the name of their god. They cried out from morning until evening. At noon Elijah began to taunt them and so they shouted louder, but to no avail. Numerical strength, earnestness and enthusiasm are not necessarily signs that something is true. To receive an answer from God you need to believe in a living God.

Then it was Elijah's turn. What was he thinking at this crucial moment? Could his prayer possibly fail? Elijah believed in a God of miracles and so he prayed with confidence. First and foremost he desired that God's name would be glorified and then that sinners would be saved. His earnest prayer had great power and wonderful results: 'The fire of the LORD fell and burned up the sacrifice, the wood, the stones and the soil, and also licked up the water in the trench.' Those who saw this supernatural fire fell prostrate and cried out, 'The LORD – he is God! The LORD – he is God!' They deserved to be consumed by this fire but were spared.

Elijah's work was not finished. Climbing to the top of Carmel, he alone persevered in prayer for the blessing of rain. His servant looked out to sea for a visible indication but there was nothing. Seven times Elijah sent him back and finally the servant saw a small cloud. That was sufficient! Immediately Ahab was told to climb into his chariot and hurry home. The sky grew black with clouds and soon heavy rain began to fall. The drought was over.

Discussion Starters

1. Why did Obadiah react as he did?

_____

_____

_____

_____

_____

2. What aspects of Ahab's character do we learn from 1 Kings 18?

_____

_____

_____

_____

_____

3. The people of Israel were in the untenable position of trying to serve both God and Baal. What lessons do we learn from this?

_____

_____

_____

_____

_____

4. The god who answers by fire – he is God. Was this an appropriate test?

_____

_____

_____

_____

_____

5. Read Job 1:16 and Revelation 13:13. Why didn't Satan send down fire in this contest between Elijah and the prophets of Baal?

_____

_____

_____

_____

6. Why did Elijah ask for many large jars of water to be poured on the offering and on the wood?

_____

_____

_____

_____

7. Elijah prayed: '… I am your servant and have done all these things at your command' (1 Kings 18:36). Why is this relevant for Christians today?

_____

_____

_____

_____

8. Elijah ordered the prophets of Baal to be executed. How would you answer those who denounce this as a barbaric act?

_____

_____

_____

_____

Personal Application

Joshua told the Israelites to forsake all traces of idolatry that might still remain among them. They were to decide whether to serve the Lord wholeheartedly. If this seemed undesirable then they could choose whom to serve. Would this be the gods their ancestors served beyond the Euphrates? Or the gods of the Amorites in whose land they then lived? A choice had to be made. However Israel decided, Joshua and his household would serve the Lord (Josh. 24:14–15).

Likewise, Elijah called for a decision when he said to the people, 'How long will you waver between two opinions? If the LORD is God, follow him; but if Baal is God, follow him' (1 Kings 18:21).

The most important decision that anyone can make is to seek God's forgiveness. Jesus said, 'I am the way and the truth and the life. No-one comes to the Father except through me' (John 14:6).

Seeing Jesus in the Scriptures

Jesus declared that there are only two roads in life (Matt. 7:13–14). One is narrow and leads to life. The other is broad and leads to destruction. Which of these two is by far the most favoured route? Jesus said it is the latter. Human nature prefers what is broad, easy access, to what is narrow and restricted. Hence, being a Christian is difficult, for our natural instinct is to follow the multitude rather than the minority. Beware of anyone who will lead you astray.

WEEK 4

Afraid and Depressed

Opening Icebreaker

A characteristic of the Bible is that it tells us not only the virtues but also the vices of its heroes. Identify some of the major weaknesses displayed by the great servants of God. Discuss how this might influence us.

Bible Readings

- 1 Kings 19:1–18
- Jonah 4:8

Opening Our Eyes

Elijah's triumph on Mount Carmel is immediately followed by tragedy. Having courageously challenged hundreds of false prophets he was then afraid of one woman. He ran for his life, taking his servant with him. At Beersheba, Elijah left his servant, went a day's journey into the desert, sat down under a broom tree and prayed that he might die. How are we to explain such utter fear and despair? Elijah, James tells us, 'was a man just like us'. Hence, it will be helpful to examine the reasons for his failure at a time when we should have expected him to succeed.

Physical, mental and spiritual fatigue were responsible for the remarkable reversal in his life. Elijah had run, ahead of Ahab's chariot, all the way to Jezreel. Prior to that he had worked extremely hard and physically he was exhausted. Furthermore, he was mentally frustrated. He realised that despite all his miraculous efforts, Jezebel was still powerful. Nothing appeared to have changed. However, the major cause of Elijah's problem was spiritual. He had made the mistake of looking away from God and this resulted in inconsistent behaviour. The man who was afraid of dying now prays that he might die. Obviously the intense loneliness of leadership and the unrelenting spiritual warfare was too much for him and he urgently needed help.

Those who are worried often neglect the basic necessities of life. They don't sleep well and they have little, or no, appetite for food. Therefore, God first provided Elijah with rest, refreshment and reassurance (1 Kings 19:5–8). As a result he was strong enough to walk the long journey to Horeb (also known as Mount Sinai), the mountain of God. Probably Elijah expected that God would meet him there as He had with Moses (Exod. 3). Later, following the people's idolatry with the golden calf, God again revealed Himself to Moses (Exod. 32 and 33). For this reason, might He not also answer Elijah's dilemma?

God didn't desert Elijah in his time of need but made him reassess his position. 'What are you doing here, Elijah?' Is this a strong rebuke? Many writers wrongly suggest that it is. When dealing with people who are seriously depressed, it's usually inadvisable to give them a stern lecture. It doesn't help, whilst constructive listening does. God knew what Elijah was thinking and that he needed to talk so as to release his inner tensions. What a privilege it is to release all our worries to God in prayer.

Elijah despondently appraised his life's work. Why, he thought, had he been such a failure? What would God do in this desperate situation? Elijah was instructed to leave the cave and stand upon the mountain. Once outside, there was a powerful wind, an earthquake and then fire, but the Lord was not in these. Elijah experienced a display of God's almighty power followed by a gentle whisper. Although Elijah believed that it was time to quit, God had other plans. Elijah was to go back and anoint Elisha to be his successor. Furthermore, Elijah did not know that there were 7,000 in Israel who hadn't worshipped Baal. A problem associated with depression is that you feel you are the only person ever to have experienced such a situation. It isn't true because there's nothing new under the sun. However desperate our situation might be, God knows how to deal with us.

Discussion Starters

1. Elijah had seen God perform many mighty miracles, yet he was afraid and depressed. What do we learn from this?

_____

_____

_____

_____

_____

2. Why did Elijah fear the threat of one woman? How can we conquer fear?

_____

_____

_____

_____

_____

3. Jezebel vowed that she would have Elijah killed because of what he had done to her prophets. Is a threat often more intimidating than the action itself?

_____

_____

_____

_____

_____

4. In Acts 20:24, Paul stated, '... I consider my life worth nothing to me, if only I may finish the race and complete the task the Lord Jesus has given me ...' How do we develop the ability to persevere?

_____

_____

_____

_____

_____

5. Elijah dismissed his servant even though he needed someone to share the burden. Why is fellowship especially important in times of despair?

_____

_____

_____

_____

_____

6. The journey to Horeb took exactly forty days and forty nights. Are there any lessons to be learnt from this?

_____

_____

_____

_____

7. Recall an occasion when you have apparently failed. In the light of this passage, what do you think of the way you responded?

_____

_____

_____

_____

8. Elijah said, 'I am no better than my ancestors' (1 Kings 19:4). How can comparing ourselves to others be dangerous?

_____

_____

_____

_____

Personal Application

The loss of a loved one, divorce, redundancy, various forms of abuse or apparent failure can lead to irrational behaviour. None of us are immune to physical, mental or spiritual fatigue. Intense feelings of anger, disappointment, guilt, sadness and tiredness are common symptoms. Sometimes a person may feel worthless, even suicidal, and it may be necessary to see a trained counsellor. What else can be done? First, it is wise to seek help from Christian friends. At times, being alone can be beneficial, but not in such situations as these. Contact with others means that it is unnecessary to bare burdens alone. Also focusing upon God's Word and frequent prayer will reveal that the problems we face are never insurmountable. If God is for us we have nothing to fear. Victory is certainly on our side.

Seeing Jesus in the Scriptures

Jesus personally experienced anguish as He considered His imminent fate on the cross. The scene was a grove called Gethsemane situated on the Mount of Olives. Here Jesus, who on this occasion had taken with Him Peter, James and John for companionship, fell with His face to the ground. He prayed, 'My Father, if it is possible, may this cup be taken from me. Yet not as I will, but as you will' (Matt. 26:39). He took refuge in prayer and persisted, finding the strength to continue with His mission.

WEEK 5

Naboth's Vineyard

Opening Icebreaker

Ahab, despite all his wealth, was discontent. In contrast, Paul could say, '... I have learned to be content whatever the circumstances' (Phil. 4:11). Consider how it is possible to find true peace and contentment in life.

Bible Readings

- 1 Kings 21:1–29
- 1 Kings 22:29–38
- 2 Kings 9:30–37
- Romans 6:23

Opening Our Eyes

Ahab, despite all his wealth, was discontent. He saw a vineyard adjoining the royal palace which he wanted, and must have, whatever the cost. It belonged to a man called Naboth and Ahab assumed, like many people, tha everything had its price. Surely Naboth would gladly par with it in exchange for a better vineyard or money. To h surprise, Naboth refused both and Ahab behaved like a spo child. He went home, lay on his bed and refused to eat.

Every spoilt person needs someone to spoil them, and Ahab had Jezebel, his wife. She believed her husband did not have to take 'No' for an answer from one of his subjects. Jezebel would get the vineyard for him. To do this she deviously arranged to have two scoundrels accu: Naboth, in public, of the capital offence of cursing God and the king. Ironically, having tried to rid the nation of the knowledge of the true God, she now accuses Naboth of cursing that God. Her plan worked perfectly. Naboth was dragged outside the city and stoned to death. To de: with the problem of inheritance, Naboth's sons were also executed (2 Kings 9:26). Evil appeared to have triumphe

Naboth had the dilemma of having to choose between obeying God or pleasing Ahab. He chose his God and was brutally murdered. Would it not have been wise to sell the vineyard? The price was generous and Ahab's request appears reasonable. What then was the problem? God's Law stipulated that landowners were not to part with the land allotted to their fathers except in cases of extreme necessity (Lev. 25:23; Num. 36:7). That is why Naboth reacts as he does. 'The LORD forbid that I should give you the inheritance of my fathers' (1 Kings 21:3). Naboth obeyed the written Word of God whereas Ahab cared only for his own immediate pleasure. He had no respect for the commandments of God.

God was not oblivious to this situation. He told Elijah, who we haven't seen for some time, to confront Ahab and tell him of the disgraceful death he and his descendants faced. It was a fearful judgment. As a result, Ahab tore his clothing, dressed in sackcloth and fasted. Was this sorrow genuine? The overall evidence would suggest that it was superficial because of what he failed to do. He did nothing to repudiate his wicked wife or eradicate her evil influence in the kingdom. He said of Micaiah, a true prophet of the Lord: '... I hate him because he never prophesies anything good about me, but always bad' (1 Kings 22:8). This clearly indicates that he had not repented. He feared judgment and wanted to avoid it, but he did not hate his sin.

Ahab died just as Elijah had said. In a battle at Ramoth Gilead, someone randomly shot an arrow which hit Ahab between the joints of his armour, and he bled to death. Then the dogs licked up his blood (1 Kings 22:29–38). All the male descendants of Ahab died (2 Kings 9:24–26; 10:1–17) and Jezebel herself was destroyed (2 Kings 9:30–37). God did all that He had said because the punishment of unrepentant sin is inevitable.

Because of sin, Ahab and his family experienced death and eternal punishment. Likewise, all who are not Christians will experience the same fate. Those who are in Christ have been made right with God. Their physical death is the door to a glorious future and everlasting life.

Discussion Starters

1. Think of some Bible characters who had to choose between compliance with human law and obedience to God's law.

_____

_____

_____

_____

_____

2. When can a Christian justify civil disobedience?

_____

_____

_____

_____

_____

3. Often one sin leads to another. Identify some of the sins committed by Ahab and Jezebel in 1 Kings 21.

_____

_____

_____

_____

_____

4. Naboth was dragged outside the city and stoned to death. What is the significance of this for us?

_____

_____

_____

_____

_____

5. Why was Elijah sent to Ahab rather than Jezebel? Wasn't she responsible for Naboth's death?

_____

_____

_____

_____

6. Ahab regarded Elijah as his enemy. Why was this?

_____

_____

_____

_____

7. What are the signs of true repentance?

_____

_____

_____

_____

8. If Ahab's repentance was false, why did God decide to delay judgment?

_____

_____

_____

_____

Personal Application

As human beings we are generally inclined to want more. This is not necessarily wrong. However, the tenth commandment (Exod. 20:17) reminds us not to wrongly desire anything that belongs to our neighbour. Do we sometimes, like Ahab, sulk if we cannot have what we want? Covetousness causes us to think only of ourselves and go after things we should not have. Do our actions ever cause injury or wrong to others? How do we react towards today's victims of injustice?

Seeing Jesus in the Scriptures

Someone in a crowd said, 'Teacher, tell my brother to divide the inheritance with me.' Jesus replied, 'Watch out! Be on your guard against all kinds of greed; a man's life does not consist in the abundance of his possessions' (Luke 12:15). In order to emphasise this point, Jesus continued by telling a parable about a certain rich man who thought only of himself. Do we, likewise, have a greedy desire for earthly possessions? Or, do we experience joy in giving, in helping others less fortunate than ourselves? Anyone is a fool to store up earthly things, but not have a rich relationship with God.

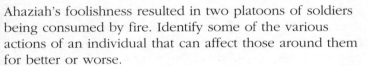

WEEK 6

Fire from Heaven

Opening Icebreaker

Ahaziah's foolishness resulted in two platoons of soldiers being consumed by fire. Identify some of the various actions of an individual that can affect those around them for better or worse.

Bible Readings

- 2 Kings 1:1–18
- Luke 9:51–56

Opening Our Eyes

How can a God of love twice send down fire from
heaven and destroy an army captain and his company of
fifty men? Surely God is not like that! Or is He? It must
be remembered that God is also a God of wrath and
will not share His supremacy with anyone. This fact is
well illustrated by the life of Ahaziah, who succeeded his
father on the throne of Israel. Like Ahab, he worshipped
the gods of his mother and so provoked the anger of Go
(1 Kings 22:51–53).

Having reigned for less than two years he suffered a fall
at his palace in Samaria. How this happened or why,
Scripture does not say. Whatever the cause, he was
seriously injured. As a result he sent messengers to the
temple of Baal-Zebub, the god of Ekron, to ask whether
he would recover from his injury. Seeking guidance
from a pagan god was a blatant rejection of Israel's God.
So Elijah, sent by God, rebuked the king through his
messengers and told him that he would certainly die.
How would Ahaziah react to this terrible news?

Ahaziah was surprised by the swift return of his
messengers. There was no way that they could have
journeyed to Ekron in Philistia and back so quickly. From
their account he soon realised that they had met Elijah
and was incensed upon hearing the prophet's message.
Hence, a captain with fifty soldiers was sent to arrest
Elijah. Did Ahaziah really think that this would answer
his problem? He was fighting against God and therefore
could not win. Whatever the number of soldiers, their
strength would have been inadequate against the almight
power of the living God. For this reason, the first troop
that was sent to seize God's prophet was consumed by
fire from heaven. A second troop suffered the same fate,
and a third one was spared only after the captain pleaded
with Elijah. At this point divine intervention told him to

accompany the soldiers back to their king. When at last they met, Elijah repeated his previous prophecy. Ahaziah would not recover from his injuries. And he didn't! 'He died, according to the word of the LORD that Elijah had spoken' (2 Kings 1:17). Ahaziah died childless and is succeeded by his brother Joram – not to be confused with Jehoram, King of Judah, who reigned at the same time.

The little we know of Ahaziah enables us to see how inconceivably hard the human heart can be. He had the written Word of God which clearly states that the sin of idolatry would be severely punished. Not only that, he should have learnt from the already fulfilled prophecies of Elijah concerning the land of Israel and his father. Despite all this he served Baal, just as his parents had done.

God would have been justified in sending immediate judgment upon Ahaziah, but He is slow to anger and abounding in love. Graciously God continues to speak to him in several ways. The nation of Moab declared its independence from Israel. Why didn't he seek the Lord's guidance as to why his kingdom was beginning to disintegrate? How did he react when seriously injured? Tragically, even on his deathbed, he continued to defy God. He died as he had lived, rejecting the constant appeals from God to alter his ways. This is a warning to us all.

Discussion Starters

1. Elijah twice called fire down from heaven to destroy men. Does this have a message for us, and, if so, what is it?

_____

_____

_____

_____

_____

2. Some people suggest that destructive fire from heaven and a God of love are incompatible. How would you answer them?

_____

_____

_____

_____

3. Ahaziah sent messengers to the temple of Baal-Zebub to ask whether he would recover. What should we see as corresponding actions today?

_____

_____

_____

_____

_____

4. In what ways might people deny or attempt to destroy God's message?

_____

_____

_____

_____

_____

5. How did the attitude of the third captain differ from that of his predecessors? What can we learn from what he does?

_____
_____
_____
_____
_____

6. How are people stubborn towards God?

_____
_____
_____
_____
_____

7. Should the fear of death have encouraged Ahaziah to be faithful to God? How do you support your answer?

_____
_____
_____
_____
_____

8. How will I be able to face the judgment of God?

_____
_____
_____
_____
_____

Personal Application

Surely Ahaziah would be intelligent enough to learn from the mistakes of his father and the fearful consequences of idolatry. Yet, sadly, he learned nothing and was indifferent to the fate of his servants. The human heart can become increasingly hard, like that of Pharaoh (Exod. 7:13,22). Ahaziah did not like God's message and so he would send his soldiers and destroy the messenger. How foolish to challenge the absolute sovereignty of God. The sixteenth-century Scottish Reformer John Knox said, 'A man with God is always in the majority.' Paul wrote, 'I can do everything through him who gives me strength' (Phil. 4:13). If God is for us it matters not who is against us.

Seeing Jesus in the Scriptures

Once John and his brother James asked if fire should be called down from heaven to destroy a Samaritan community because of their inhospitable attitude towards Jesus (Luke 9:51–56). Probably they were thinking of Elijah (2 Kings 1:10,12). However, what is right in one situation can be wrong in another. Hence, in this instance, Jesus rebuked them, and they went to another village. To destroy the Samaritans because of a single act of discourtesy could not be justified. They had not hardened their hearts as Ahab and Ahaziah did, for we later see that many of them believed Philip as he preached the good news of Jesus Christ (Acts 8:5–8).

WEEK 7

A Time of Transition

Opening Icebreaker

Elijah was a man just like us. He experienced great success followed by the depths of despair and depression. How is this relevant for members of the group?

Bible Readings

- 1 Kings 19:19–21
- 2 Kings 2:1–18
- James 5:17–18

Opening Our Eyes

The imminent departure of Elijah from this world was widely anticipated. Prophets at Bethel and Jericho, as well as Elisha, were aware that he would be taken away that day (2 Kings 2:3,5). Elijah was prepared to make his farewell journey alone but Elisha repeatedly insisted on accompanying him. This persistence ensured that he witnessed both the ascension and the sign of succession.

Leaving the prophets behind, the two men reached the River Jordan. The prophets watched from a distance as Elijah folded his cloak and struck the water with it. The river divided and the two of them walked across on dry ground. This river had been parted before so as to allow the children of Israel to reach the promised land (Josh. 3:14–17). The Jordan turned back (Psa. 114:3), and the Israelites walked forward on dry ground.

Just prior to his miraculous transition Elijah asked Elisha, 'What can I do for you before I am taken from you?' How would you react to such a question from a man who could work miracles! Would you ask for health or wealth or fame? Your answer will be a true revelation of your character. Without hesitation Elisha requested that he might be Elijah's rightful successor. He valued being a man of God above everything else. Of course, what he asked for was difficult for Elijah. Only God could grant such a request. The test would be whether or not Elisha had the ability to see and understand the spiritual world. He soon received an answer for suddenly their conversation was interrupted by the appearance of a chariot of fire drawn by horses of fire. It separated them and Elijah was carried by a whirlwind into heaven. Then there was silence. All that remained was the cloak of Elijah.

Several years previous, Elijah had found Elisha ploughing. He went over to him and, without saying a word, threw his coat across the young man's shoulders. Then he walked away (1 Kings 19:19–21). Elisha understood the significance of this. It was seen as a symbol of succession. Now God threw the coat at Elisha's feet. He picked it up and returned to the bank of the River Jordan. Was he really going to take over from Elijah? Could he divide the river using the cloak? In itself the cloak had no power but the God of Elijah did. That is why Elisha asked, 'Where now is the LORD, the God of Elijah?' He didn't ask where Elijah was. He was gone, but God remained and Elisha's request was fulfilled. The group of prophets from Jericho looking on saw what had happened and knew that Elisha had become Elijah's successor.

Elijah was a man just like us. He was a prophet, but he was not perfect. He alternated between confidence on Mount Carmel and despair on Mount Horeb. Had he been superhuman his life would have been inapplicable to ours for it would have set a standard which was impossible to emulate. Elijah was an ordinary man who could do extraordinary things because he believed in a supernatural God. Likewise, Christians today can achieve what appears to be impossible providing that they are possessed by God's Spirit. Jesus said, '… obey everything I have commanded you. And surely I am with you always, to the very end of the age' (Matt. 28:20). God can accomplish great things through faithful people.

Discussion Starters

1. The prophets said, 'Do you know that the LORD is going to take your master from you today?' Elisha replied, 'Yes I know … but do not speak of it' (2 Kings 2:3,5). Why should they remain silent?

2. How did Elijah occupy his final hours on earth?

3. Why did Elijah repeatedly encourage Elisha to leave him?

4. Elisha said to Elijah, 'Let me inherit a double portion of your spirit' (2 Kings 2:9). What did he mean by this request?

5. Why did Elijah find the above request difficult?

_____

_____

_____

_____

_____

6. Read 1 Kings 19:4. How does 2 Kings 2:1–12 reveal that God's plan is best for our lives?

_____

_____

_____

_____

_____

7. What practical lessons do we learn from the accomplishments of Elijah?

_____

_____

_____

_____

_____

8. Where now is the Lord the God of Elijah?

_____

_____

_____

_____

_____

Personal Application

The return of Elijah was, and still is, a part of Jewish belief. This assumption is clearly based on Scripture. 'See, I will send you the prophet Elijah before that great and dreadful day of the LORD comes' (Mal. 4:5). Nevertheless, Elijah in this instance is not to be thought of as Elijah in person, but of another called John the Baptist. He, himself, denied that he was Elijah in person (John 1:21) but Jesus said he was the promised Elijah (Matt. 11:14; 17:11–13). John would be a forerunner of Jesus, preparing the people for His arrival. The message of Elijah and John is as relevant today as it was then: turn from your sins and turn to God.

Seeing Jesus in the Scriptures

Jesus led Peter, James and John up a high mountain. There Jesus was transfigured before them. His face shone like the sun, and His clothing became as brilliant as the light. Then the disciples saw Moses and Elijah talking with Jesus of His departure which He was about to bring to fulfilment at Jerusalem (Luke 9:28–36).

Why were Moses and Elijah chosen for this sublime occasion? The probable answer is that they represented respectively the Law and the Prophets, both of which Jesus had come to fulfil (Matt. 5:17). His ministry was not contrary to the Old Testament but in agreement with it; indeed without Jesus it was unfulfilled. In Jesus, God has come in person to reconcile a rebellious world. Hence, listen to what God the Spirit is saying through God the Son!

Leader's Notes

Week 1: God Provides for His People

Opening Icebreaker

The aim of this exercise is to emphasise that pleasures, possessions and prestige continually beckon us to come and serve them.

Aim of the Session

To show that we can expect God's provision only when we are following Him in obedience.

Discussion Starters

1. To experience God's guidance we must trust Him to lead us and realise our own limitations. Then He will direct our paths (Prov. 3:5–6). Through studying the Bible and earnest prayer we can confidently seek His will (1 John 5:14–15). It should be stressed that true prayer must be founded on the theme 'your will be done' (Matt. 6:10). Even Jesus submitted Himself entirely to the will of His Father (Matt. 26:39).

2. Obedience to God is to submit to His standards, rather than our own. It is a visible expression of our love to do His will. Jesus said, 'If you love me, you will obey what I command' (John 14:15). This is proof of genuine discipleship. Obedience to religious laws alone is not the means of securing God's favour; it must include our grateful response to His forgiveness through Jesus Christ.

3. Abram received God's call to leave his country, his people and his father's household and go to an unknown land (Gen. 12:1). He was to commence a journey and rely on God to lead him each step of the way. If he had not responded to the call he would not have known the blessing of God. Likewise it is essential that we are in the

place where God wants us to be. Then He will provide for all our needs.

4. Occasionally loneliness can be self-inflicted. A person isolates themselves so that there is no one to help in times of need (Eccl. 4:9–10). Alternatively, circumstances may mean that, like Elijah, we have to learn to be alone with God. Sometimes it is beneficial to be alone as Jesus was (Matt. 14:23). Although people might desert us, we are assured that Jesus will be with us always (Matt. 28:20).

5. For Elijah to go to Zarephath, an area ruled by Jezebel's father, involved a difficult journey. Why go there? Surely God could sustain him anywhere. Neither was the move primarily to provide him with human companionship. If that were so, he could have gone to one of the widows in Israel (Luke 4:25–26). God had chosen this widow before she was ever aware of it to trust Him (1 Kings 17:9). Her conversion clearly reveals God's sovereignty in the process of salvation.

6. Probably God's plan appeared strange to Elijah. For example, he had to depend upon a woman whereas normally the man would provide. In addition, she was a Gentile whilst he was a Jew. He was commanded to take help from someone who didn't belong to the people of God. Not a likely candidate, but God uses the most unlikely people to do His work.

7. Elijah's request for a cake of bread can appear to be selfish considering the widow's dire circumstances. Even so, the demand is made, but it is followed by a promise of sufficient food until the famine ends. What a test of faith! Willingly she did as Elijah commanded and was rewarded. The gospel confronts us with the same demand: namely, to put God first. Those who do, discover that He provides their daily bread.

3. Jesus tells us that there is no need to worry about food, drink or clothing (Matt. 6:31–34). To do so would be a sign of unbelief from anyone who knows what their heavenly Father can and will do.

Our deepest need is met by Christ Himself. 'I am the bread of life' (John 6:35,48). 'I am the living bread …' (John 6:51). He is the all-sufficient sustenance of life.

Week 2: The Widow's Son

Opening Icebreaker
The aim of this exercise is to see how unrighteous anger can make us act in ways that we later regret whilst righteous anger arises from our devotion to God and compassion for others.

Aim of the Session
To understand why God allows challenges in our lives and how we should deal with them.

Discussion Starters
1. Stephen was stoned to death (Acts 7:59–60). John the Baptist was beheaded (Matt. 14:1–10) and James died by the sword (Acts 12:2). Christians have been tortured, even to the point of death, throughout the centuries. Certainly, Christians are saved from the penalty of sin but not from suffering.

2. The idea that personal disaster is the result of personal sin was a common belief amongst the Jews (Job 4:7; John 9:2). However, Jesus says that this is not necessarily true (Luke 13:1–5). Books such as Job and Ecclesiastes also clearly reveal that punishment can be disproportionate to the crime. It is a fact that in this life the wicked frequently prosper whilst the righteous suffer.

3. Our circumstances would sometimes seem to contradict what God has promised. This is because much of the future is hidden from us. Hence, we may not understand now, or in our lifetime, why certain things happen. It is not for us to question the ways of God but rather to accept that He never fails to keep a promise.

4. Many of our problems are caused by us looking away from God. Elijah when faced with the threat of Jezebel saw only a furious woman and, in panic, ran. Peter made the same mistake whilst walking on the water. As soon as his eyes were captivated by the high waves he began to sink. His faith gave way to fright (Matt. 14:30). Our limitations should remind us to keep our eyes upon Jesus.

5. When her only son died the distraught widow reacted by criticising Elijah and his God. Then she blamed herself. It appeared to be a hopeless and irreversible situation. Elijah, although concerned and bewildered by the boy's death, remained calm. Neither did he try to justify himself or God. Instead Elijah did the only thing that he could do in such a situation. He prayed on the basis of God's promise.

6. God appears to have taken the life of one He had promised to sustain until the famine was over (1 Kings 17:14). Therefore, even though the boy had died, Elijah was confident that God would act. He prayed fervently on the basis of God's promise, like others before him (Gen. 32:11–12; Deut. 9:25-29). Abraham had found himself in a similar situation (Gen. 22:1–19). Although this was a severe test, he was confident that his son Isaac would survive the ordeal (Heb. 11:17–19).

7. God always hears our prayers, but He may deny our requests. Elijah experienced this when he prayed that he might die, for God had another plan. Elijah did not know that someday a whirlwind would carry him straight from earth into heaven without his dying. God knows what is

best for us and so we must expect Him to refuse some of our requests. That is why even Elijah didn't get everything he prayed for.

8. Despite the miraculous daily provision of food, Elijah's witness appeared to be ineffective until the boy died. Then arose the opportunity to display the love and almighty power of his God. This first example in the Bible of revival from death brought one woman to personally know the Lord (1 Kings 17:24). Furthermore, Elijah realised that with God there is no problem which is too great.

Week 3: Conflict on Carmel

Opening Icebreaker
This exercise is to stress that our prayers should be driven by a strong inward necessity. Prayers should be fervent, persistent and expectant, and to be successful must be according to God's will.

Aim of the Session
To see why it is necessary to accept the absolute and universal supremacy of the true and living God.

Discussion Starters
1. Many people consider Obadiah to be one of the great enigmas of the Bible. He was a devout man of God and also a trusted servant of the vile Ahab. Undoubtedly he had a fear of God and a fear of man. That is why he was reluctant to do as Elijah commanded. It is always easier to talk about courage than to display it. Obadiah, despite his weaknesses, aimed to live a godly life in a very corrupt society.

2. When Jezebel murdered God's servants, Ahab did not intervene. He had concern neither for God or his subjects.

They were starving but he was more concerned about grass for his animals. The major revelation of his character is the malice shown towards Elijah when these two meet. Ahab was in no doubt as to who was responsible for the drought. He was oblivious to the clear teachings of God.

3. There is a danger that we attempt to offer God a shared or secondary place in our lives. Such an attitude is unacceptable to God (Exod. 20:3). We are either for Him or against Him. It is impossible for us to devote ourselves fully to two things at once (Matt. 6:24). Hence, let us not waver between various options. Being a Christian involves total surrender to the one true living God.

4. Baal was the storm-god who sent the lightning and the rain. Therefore, it would be difficult for the prophets of Baal to reject Elijah's appropriate challenge.

'For the LORD your God is a consuming fire, a jealous God' were words spoken by Moses to deter Israel from idolatry (Deut. 4:24). On Mount Carmel God publicly burned up the sacrifice. The fire of God consumes or it consecrates depending upon whether you are a sinner or a saint (Matt. 13:40–43).

5. Satan, despite being able to perform great and miraculous signs, could not send down fire from heaven. In this instance God would not permit it because this was a direct challenge between Himself and Baal as to who was the true God. Satan does nothing without the permission of God (Job 1:12; 2:6).

6. Twelve large jars of water were poured over the offering and the wood so that they were soaked. The water ran down around the altar and even overflowed the trench Elijah had dug. There was no possibility of ignition by human means. Hence, the people were to be in no doubt that the origin of this fire was supernatural. They

were to know for certain that it was not Elijah but God who was responsible.

7. Elijah worked according to God's plan and so he had every reason to be confident that God would answer his faith by fire, as He had done for others in the past (Judg. 6:17–21; 1 Chron. 21:26). Elijah was not testing God but praying on the basis of God's revealed truth. Likewise, Christian faith is to believe what God has said and then with steadfast endurance claim His promises.

8. If the prophets of Baal had been allowed to escape they would have exposed Israel to further corruption. Their death was inevitable because it was a necessary act in the history of redemption. Since Jesus came into the world the situation has changed. New Testament passages such as John 3 and Hebrews 10 show that holiness is now obtained through His death and resurrection, not through eradicating those who offend God.

Week 4: Afraid and Depressed

Opening Icebreaker

Consider examples such as the drunkenness of Noah (Gen. 9:21); the temper of Moses (Exod. 2:12); the lust of David and its aftermath (2 Sam. 11:1–17); and the denial of Peter (Matt. 26:69–75). The great servants of God were human beings, just as we are.

Aim of the Session

To appreciate the great danger we face in looking away from God.

Discussion Starters

1. Past successes do not prevent future failures. Any attempt to do God's work by our own strength rather

than working in the power of the Holy Spirit, will inevitably fail. We must be constantly conscious of our weakness and aware of God's omnipotence. Elijah experienced burnout and as a result only looked at the difficulties. God graciously invites us to unburden ourselves (Matt. 11:28–30).

2. Elijah's tiredness was followed by depression which, in turn, caused him to run into the wilderness. This was because his eyes were focused upon Jezebel and her murderous threats. He had lost sight of the promises, power and protection of God. Christians, like Elijah, can become tired of the unrelenting struggle against evil. Nevertheless, if God be for us, it matters not who is against us (Phil. 4:13).

3. Jezebel sent a messenger to Elijah to announce his imminent death. Why not kill him immediately? Sometimes the threat of death can be more intimidating than the action itself. Certainly Elijah, the previously invincible man of God, ran for his life.

Shemaiah tried to induce fear in the heart of Nehemiah, but without success (Neh. 6:10–11). Nehemiah, like the apostles, feared God, rather than men (Acts 5:29).

4. Christmas Evans, a British evangelist, once said, 'I'd rather burn out than rust out in the service of the Lord.' Some Christians work on the same principle today, unlike Paul, and fail to maintain an effective ministry over the long term. It is impossible to successfully live the Christian life without times of rest and spiritual renewing. Our Lord Himself required this and intended it for His followers (Mark 6:30–31).

5. Elijah desperately needed help and yet he dismissed his only servant. Self-pity has a way of making you isolate yourself from other people. It is also possible to

e lonely in a crowd. I regularly meet active Christians, specially leaders, who are lonely. Whether single or married, it is essential to develop a small group of close riendships. Only then can you grow as a person and hare your burdens.

. Forty is a number associated with the story of Moses Exod. 24:18; Num. 14:33–34). Whilst walking to Mount Horeb, Elijah would relate his situation to that of his ncestors. They had refused to enter the land of Canaan nd many had died in the wilderness. God appeared o have failed until He raised up a new generation and inally brought them into the promised land. This was reminder for Elijah, then in that same wilderness, to persevere despite his trials.

. Elijah had experienced remarkable success in his ife. Irrespective of this he considered himself to be a complete failure. He wanted to die. Despite the triumph on Mount Carmel, the problem of false worship continued nd Jezebel was still powerful. It appeared to Elijah that his hard work had achieved nothing worthwhile. He was tired of the relentless struggle. When Christians feel empted to give up, it helps to look carefully at the life of esus who is our source of rest and strength (Heb. 12:3).

. It is unhelpful to compare oneself to other people. An attitude of superiority results in pride, whilst a feeling of nferiority leads to envy. Only a self-examination before God reveals that 'there is no-one righteous, not even one' Rom. 3:10). Inherently I am no better than my ancestors.

Week 5: Naboth's Vineyard

Opening Icebreaker
To show that true peace and contentment in life are found only in a close relationship with the Lord.

Aim of the Session
To consider what can happen when the secular and the godly collide.

Discussion Starters
1. There are many instances within the Bible of civil disobedience. For example, when Pharaoh told the Hebrew midwives to kill the newborn boys, they did not obey (Exod. 1:17). Obadiah secretly protected the Lord's prophets (1 Kings 18:4). Shadrach, Meshach and Abednego refused to worship the image of gold (Dan. 3). Daniel refused to obey the decree issued by King Darius, even though this was state policy for only thirty days (Dan. 6). In the New Testament we see that when the Sanhedrin commanded the apostles not to witness in the name of Jesus, they refused to comply (Acts 4:18–20; 5:29).

2. When it is a question of choosing between other people and obeying God, there should be no doubt as to what course to take. Christians, whilst always aiming to be law-abiding citizens, must maintain their ultimate allegiance to the kingdom of God (Acts 4:19). It should be noted that civil disobedience is only appropriate after all legal means of correcting an unjust situation have been exhausted. Also, as far as it depends on any Christian involved, all action must be peaceful.

3. The twenty-first chapter of 1 Kings begins with greed in Ahab's heart. He saw a vineyard and was determined to own it whatever the cost. Jezebel would get it for him by writing letters in which there is deliberate hypocrisy: 'Proclaim a day of fasting …' (v.9). Also there is slander

gainst Naboth, for the ninth commandment against
earing false witness (Deut. 5:20) does not deter Jezebel.
his is then followed by pre-meditated murder and theft.

. Obeying God does not mean that we shall never
uffer. In fact, the true follower of Christ cannot escape
ersecution (2 Tim. 3:12). Anyone who accepts standards
which are different from the world's is certain to
ncounter trouble.

. Jezebel did not directly involve Ahab in the murder
f Naboth. She wrote letters in his name without telling
im the contents. Even so, God held Ahab primarily
esponsible for several reasons. For example, Ahab
vas a Jew whilst Jezebel was a Gentile. He knew the
en Commandments of God and realised that many of
nem had been broken. He was the king and therefore
bove the queen and all his subjects. Also, it was Ahab's
ovetousness that was responsible for this terrible chain
f events.

. Those who love sin invariably loathe the truth and
nyone who proclaims it. Thus, Ahab considered Elijah
nd Micaiah, both prophets of God, to be his enemies
1 Kings 21:20; 22:8). In reality enemies are those who
eep the truth from us by claiming that repentance is
nnecessary for sinners to be saved.

. True repentance will always evidence itself by being
orry for sin and by being devoted to a new way of life,
erving God. It is not enough to say that we believe in
od (James 2:14–26). There must be an inner change,
change of heart, which expresses itself outwardly
y producing fruit in keeping with repentance
Matt. 3:8). This will be manifest by characteristics such
s generosity, honesty, thoughtfulness and contentment
Luke 3:11–14).

8. By withholding judgment God was demonstrating the greatness of His mercy. God is slow to anger and abounding in love (Psa. 103:8; 145:8). However, a day will arrive when the opportunity to be saved will be withdrawn.

Week 6: Fire from Heaven

Opening Icebreaker
To show that challenges are opportunities to grow spiritually, to become more Christlike (James 1:2–4). You should not be discouraged by the size of the challenge but rather encouraged by the power of God (1 Sam. 17:41–47). It is possible for us to be the instruments of God's victory.

Aim of the Session
To emphasise the fact that those who ignore God's Word will one day perish.

Discussion Starters
1. The repeated destruction by fire (2 Kings 1:10,12) reveals that ultimately the Word of God will prevail. Temporal judgments are, today, a foreboding reminder to any who reject Jesus Christ. Those who do not repent will certainly perish (Matt. 13:41–42; Rev. 20:15).

2. God is a God of love (John 3:16). He is also a God of holiness (Lev. 11:44–45) and therefore a God of wrath (Rom. 1:18). Hence, will God punish or pardon sin? Romans 6:23 reveals that He can do both and if that appears to be a contradiction to anyone, it is because they do not understand the true meaning of the cross.

3. Many millions of people consult their horoscopes every day in the newspapers and magazines. They believe that the stars and the planets determine the course of human

fe. Surely if people know the future they can be better
repared to handle it. This explains its popularity even
hough it is contrary to the teaching of the Bible
Lev. 19:31; 1 Chron. 10:13). God alone can enable us to
ce the future with confidence.

. It is not unusual to hear statements such as: 'Yes, I
now what the Bible says but we are living in a different
ge.' Or, 'I only accept parts of the Bible to be true.'
hese, and similar attitudes, are to deny the authority of
od. All Scripture is God-inspired and therefore profitable
2 Tim. 3:16).

. The captain of the third company believed that Elijah
vas a man of God. Consequently, he came and fell on
is knees before Elijah and pleaded for his own life and
1e lives of those who were with him. Observe that,
nlike his predecessors (2 Kings 1:9,11), he says nothing
bout the word of the king. He knew that it was wrong
o challenge the Word of God. As a result he and his
ompany were spared.

. Ahaziah had been warned many times that his sin
vould be punished. He had the written Word of God. He
new of the miracles performed by Elijah and had seen
1e prophecy fulfilled concerning the death of his father.
amazingly the stubborn always remain unconvinced
y the displays of God's power. Examples are: Pharaoh
uring the time of the Exodus; the people of Israel
hroughout their history; and the Pharisees during the
me of Jesus. Likewise many people today refuse to
ccept the truth, despite the overwhelming evidence.

. Often the fear of imminent death makes people
arefully consider their spiritual state. Ahaziah was
oncerned and urgently wanted to know if he would
ecover from his injury. What he did, however, proves
1at his soul was in a worse state than his body. He

consulted Baal-Zebub, the god of Ekron. Awareness of our own mortality should encourage us not to delay in accepting the salvation Christ offers (John 8:23–24).

8. King Solomon wisely observed that 'He who conceals his sins does not prosper, but whoever confesses and renounces them finds mercy' (Prov. 28:13). Our attitude to sin must not be to deny it, but to confess it. Then, through Jesus Christ's sacrificial death we are reconciled to God (1 John 1:8–9; Rom. 5:9–11). God takes people at their own estimate, reverses that estimate, and acts accordingly (Luke 18:9–14).

Week 7: A Time of Transition

Opening Icebreaker
The aim of this exercise is not to concentrate upon the faults of Elijah so that we might try and justify our own sins. Rather it is to stress that we are totally dependent upon God for our strength. Emphasise the importance of prayer.

Aim of the Session
To reveal that God's people today may be strengthened and equipped by His Spirit.

Discussion Starters
1. Regardless of the discouragement from the prophets (2 Kings 2:3,5) Elisha persevered. He did not wish to hear the things they had to say because he realised that their attitude would be pessimistic. He would allow no one to deter him from his task. There are always people who will try and discourage us. Consequently our thoughts must be focused upon what the Bible says and the fact that God's work is ultimately going to triumph.

. Elijah took Elisha on a farewell tour to the groups of
prophets (2 Kings 2:1–6). He wanted to give these young
men, who will continue the role of reformation in Israel,
 final word of encouragement. A major responsibility of
ll Christian leaders is to help develop the gifts of others
nd to keep a close watch for those who have the ability
o succeed them.

. Elijah on his final journey repeatedly told Elisha not to
go with him (2 Kings 2:2,4,6). Each time Elisha refused,
or he is a loyal servant who is determined to go all the
way, however difficult it might be. How committed are
we to God's calling? Christians often desire to serve God,
but are they determined to love and honour Him in all
hey do (Matt. 22:37–38)?

. Elisha asked for a double portion of Elijah's spirit or
power. This does not mean that he wanted twice as much
s Elijah had, but refers to the share that by law the
irstborn son would inherit from his father (Deut. 21:17).
As firstborn he had the right and the duty to carry on
he father's name and work. Elisha's greatest desire was
o succeed Elijah, but he knew that it was impossible to
undertake such a responsibility without the Spirit of God.

. God alone can give His Spirit to anyone (1 John 3:24;
:13). Thus it was not for Elijah to grant Elisha's request.
He could only intercede for him. Then the vital test would
be if Elisha had the ability to witness the departure of his
master. He had, and his succession was confirmed. Until
our eyes are opened by the Holy Spirit, the Bible will be
of no great benefit. Like the psalmist our prayer must be:
Open my eyes that I may see the wonderful things in
our law' (Psa. 119:18).

. God's ways are so much better than ours. If God had
agreed to Elijah's request to die in the Judean wilderness, it
would have been a forlorn anti-climax to his life. We should

be thankful that God does not always grant our requests.

7. It would be wrong to think of Elijah as an extra special kind of believer. Instead we should see him as someone who displayed the features of a life of faith. He was eager, earnest and enthusiastic in serving God. He was a man of prayer. With the Spirit of God he was bold whilst by himself he was afraid and at times severely depressed.

8. People come, and people go, but God's work continues (Heb. 13:8). The Lord the God of Elijah is wherever people will faithfully act in accordance with His will. Faith, as small as a mustard seed, can achieve what appears to be impossible (Matt. 17:20). Our need is not to have great faith in God, but to have faith in a great God.

National Distributors

UK: (and countries not listed below)
CWR, Waverley Abbey House, Waverley Lane, Farnham, Surrey GU9 8EP.
Tel: (01252) 784700 Outside UK (44) 1252 784700 Email: mail@cwr.org.uk

AUSTRALIA: KI Entertainment, Unit 21 317-321 Woodpark Road, Smithfield, New South Wales 2164. Tel: 1 800 850 777 Fax: 02 9604 3699 Email: sales@kientertainment.com.au

CANADA: David C Cook Distribution Canada, PO Box 98, 55 Woodslee Avenue, Paris, Ontario N3L 3E5. Tel: 1800 263 2664 Email: swansons@cook.ca

GHANA: Challenge Enterprises of Ghana, PO Box 5723, Accra. Tel: (021) 222437/223249 Fax: (021) 226227 Email: ceg@africaonline.com.gh

HONG KONG: Cross Communications Ltd, 1/F, 562A Nathan Road, Kowloon. Tel: 2780 1188 Fax: 2770 6229 Email: cross@crosshk.com

INDIA: Crystal Communications, 10-3-18/4/1, East Marredpalli, Secunderabad – 500026, Andhra Pradesh. Tel/Fax: (040) 27737145 Email: crystal_edwj@rediffmail.com

KENYA: Keswick Books and Gifts Ltd, PO Box 10242-00400, Nairobi. Tel: (254) 20 312639/3870125 Email: keswick@swiftkenya.com

MALAYSIA: Canaanland, No. 25 Jalan PJU 1A/41B, NZX Commercial Centre, Ara Jaya, 47301 Petaling Jaya, Selangor. Tel: (03) 7885 0540/1/2 Fax: (03) 7885 0545 Email: info@canaanland.com.my

Salvation Book Centre (M) Sdn Bhd, 23 Jalan SS 2/64, 47300 Petaling Jaya, Selangor. Tel: (03) 78766411/78766797 Fax: (03) 78757066/78756360 Email: info@salvationbookcentre.com

NEW ZEALAND: KI Entertainment, Unit 21 317-321 Woodpark Road, Smithfield, New South Wales 2164, Australia. Tel: 0 800 850 777 Fax: +612 9604 3699 Email: sales@kientertainment.com.au

NIGERIA: FBFM, Helen Baugh House, 96 St Finbarr's College Road, Akoka, Lagos. Tel: (01) 7747429/4700218/825775/827264 Email: fbfm@hyperia.com

PHILIPPINES: OMF Literature Inc, 776 Boni Avenue, Mandaluyong City. Tel: (02) 531 2183 Fax: (02) 531 1960 Email: gloadlaon@omflit.com

SINGAPORE: Alby Commercial Enterprises Pte Ltd, 95 Kallang Avenue #04-00, AIS Industrial Building, 339420. Tel: (65) 629 27238 Fax: (65) 629 27235 Email: marketing@alby.com.sg

SOUTH AFRICA: Struik Christian Books, 80 MacKenzie Street, PO Box 1144, Cape Town 8000. Tel: (021) 462 4360 Fax: (021) 461 3612 Email: info@struikchristianmedia.co.za

SRI LANKA: Christombu Publications (Pvt) Ltd, Bartleet House, 65 Braybrooke Place, Colombo 2. Tel: (9411) 2421073/2447665 Email: dhanad@bartleet.com

USA: David C Cook Distribution Canada, PO Box 98, 55 Woodslee Avenue, Paris, Ontario N3L 3E5, Canada. Tel: 1800 263 2664 Email: swansons@cook.ca

CWR is a Registered Charity - Number 294387
CWR is a Limited Company registered in England - Registration Number 1990308

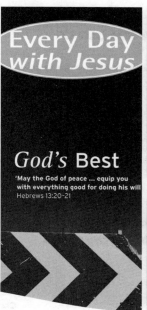

Every Day with Jesus

God's Best

'May the God of peace ... equip you
with everything good for doing his will
Hebrews 13:20-21

ransforming lives

urses and seminars

blishing and new media

nference facilities

CWR's vision is to enable people to experience
personal transformation through applying God's Word
to their lives and relationships.

Our Bible-based training and resources help people
around the world to:
• Grow in their walk with God
• Understand and apply Scripture to their lives
• Resource themselves and their church
• Develop pastoral care and counselling skills
• Train for leadership
• Strengthen relationships, marriage and family life
and much more.

WR **Applying God's Word**
to everyday life and relationships

R, Waverley Abbey House,
verley Lane, Farnham,
rey GU9 8EP, UK

ephone: +44 (0)1252 784700
ail: info@cwr.org.uk
bsite: www.cwr.org.uk

jistered Charity No 294387
mpany Registration No 1990308

Our insightful writers provide daily Bible-reading
notes and other resources for all ages, and our
experienced course designers and presenters have
gained an international reputation for excellence and
effectiveness.

CWR's Training and Conference Centre in Surrey,
England, provides excellent facilities in an idyllic setting
– ideal for both learning and spiritual refreshment.

Dramatic new resource

Acts 1–12: Church on the move
by Christine Platt

There is much we can learn from the believers in the first part of Acts. In taking the message of Jesus to 'regions beyond', we will encounter failures, successes, joys and sorrows just as they did. This challenging series will encourage you to be faithful and courageous, empowered by the same Holy Spirit as the early believers. He longs to pour out His gifts for ministry and to produce His fruit in our lives.
ISBN: 978-1-85345-574-2

Also available in the bestselling
Cover to Cover Bible Study Series

1 Corinthians
Restoring harmony
ISBN: 978-1-85345-374-8

2 Corinthians
Growing a Spirit-filled church
ISBN: 978-1-85345-551-3

1 Timothy
Healthy churches – effective Christians
ISBN: 978-1-85345-291-8

23rd Psalm
The Lord is my shepherd
ISBN: 978-1-85345-449-3

2 Timothy and Titus
Vital Christianity
ISBN: 978-1-85345-338-0

Ecclesiastes
Hard questions and spiritual answers
ISBN: 978-1-85345-371-7

Ephesians
Claiming your inheritance
ISBN: 978-1-85345-229-1

Esther
For such a time as this
ISBN: 978-1-85345-511-7

Fruit of the Spirit
Growing more like Jesus
ISBN: 978-1-85345-375-5

Genesis 1–11
Foundations of reality
ISBN: 978-1-85345-404-2

God's Rescue Plan
Finding God's fingerprints on human history
ISBN: 978-1-85345-294-9

Great Prayers of the Bible
Applying them to our lives today
ISBN: 978-1-85345-253-6

Hebrews
Jesus – simply the best
ISBN: 978-1-85345-337-3

Hosea
The love that never fails
ISBN: 978-1-85345-290-1

Isaiah 1–39
Prophet to the nations
ISBN: 978-1-85345-510-0

Isaiah 40–66
Prophet of restoration
ISBN: 978-1-85345-550-6

James
Faith in action
ISBN: 978-1-85345-293-2

Jeremiah
The passionate prophet
ISBN: 978-1-85345-372-4

John's Gospel
Exploring the seven miraculous signs
ISBN: 978-1-85345-295-6

Joseph
The power of forgiveness and reconciliation
ISBN: 978-1-85345-252-9

Mark
Life as it is meant to be lived
ISBN: 978-1-85345-233-8

The Divine Blueprint
God's extraordinary power in ordinary lives
ISBN: 978-1-85345-292-5

Moses
Face to face with God
ISBN: 978-1-85345-336-6

The Holy Spirit
Understanding and experiencing Him
ISBN: 978-1-85345-254-3

Nehemiah
Principles for life
ISBN: 978-1-85345-335-9

The Image of God
His attributes and character
ISBN: 978-1-85345-228-4

Parables
Communicating God on earth
ISBN: 978-1-85345-340-3

The Kingdom
Studies from Matthew's Gospel
ISBN: 978-1-85345-251-2

Philemon
From slavery to freedom
ISBN: 978-1-85345-453-0

The Letter to the Colossians
In Christ alone
ISBN: 978-1-85345-405-9

Philippians
Living for the sake of the gospel
ISBN: 978-1-85345-421-9

The Letter to the Romans
Good news for everyone
ISBN: 978-1-85345-250-5

Proverbs
Living a life of wisdom
ISBN: 978-1-85345-373-1

The Lord's Prayer
Praying Jesus' way
ISBN: 978-1-85345-460-8

Revelation 1-3
Christ's call to the Church
ISBN: 978-1-85345-461-5

The Prodigal Son
Amazing grace
ISBN: 978-1-85345-412-7

Revelation 4-22
The Lamb wins! Christ's final victory
ISBN: 978-1-85345-411-0

The Second Coming
Living in the light of Jesus' return
ISBN: 978-1-85345-422-6

Rivers of Justice
Responding to God's call to righteousness today
ISBN: 978-1-85345-339-7

The Sermon on the Mount
Life within the new covenant
ISBN: 978-1-85345-370-0

Ruth
Loving kindness in action
ISBN: 978-1-85345-231-4

The Tabernacle
Entering into God's presence
ISBN: 978-1-85345-230-7

The Covenants
God's promises and their relevance today
ISBN: 978-1-85345-255-0

The Uniqueness of our Faith
What makes Christianity distinctive?
ISBN: 978-1-85345-232-1

For current prices visit www.cwr.org.uk

Cover to Cover Every Day
Gain deeper knowledge of the Bible

Each issue of these bimonthly daily Bible-reading notes gives
you insightful commentary on a book of the Old and New
Testaments with reflections on a psalm each weekend by
Philip Greenslade.

Enjoy contributions from two well-known authors every
two months, and over a five-year period you will be taken
through the entire Bible.

ISSN: 1744-0114
Only £2.75 each (plus p&p)
£14.95 for annual subscription (bimonthly, p&p included in UK)
£13.80 for annual email subscription
(available from www.cwr.org.uk/store)

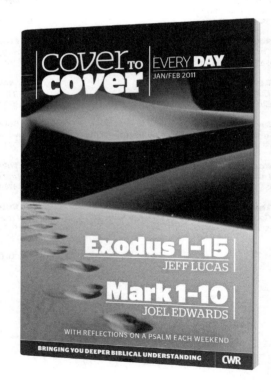